W9-AVI-410

BIBLE TRIVIA
for Every Day

Bob
Phillips

HARVEST HOUSE PUBLISHERS

EUGENE, OREGON

Unless otherwise indicated, all Scripture quotations are taken from the New King James Version. Copyright © 1982 by Thomas Nelson, Inc. Used by permission. All rights reserved.

Verses marked KJV are taken from the King James Version of the Bible.

Cover by Dugan Design Group, Bloomington, Minnesota

Cover Illustration © Dugan Design Group

BIBLE TRIVIA FOR EVERY DAY
Copyright © 2008 by Bob Phillips
Published by Harvest House Publishers
Eugene, Oregon 97402
www.harvesthousepublishers.com

ISBN-13: 978-0-7369-2320-0
ISBN-10: 0-7369-2320-9

All rights reserved. No part of this publication may be reproduced, stored in a retrieval system, or transmitted in any form or by any means—electronic, mechanical, digital, photocopy, recording, or any other—except for brief quotations in printed reviews, without the prior permission of the publisher.

Printed in the United States of America

08 09 10 11 12 13 14 / BP-SK / 10 9 8 7 6 5 4 3 2 1

Contents

✳ ✳ ✳

A Word from Bob

For a number of years I have collected unusual Bible trivia, quotations, and jokes. They have been fun to share with family and friends and to add a little sparkle to sermons.

Bible Trivia for Every Day can be used in a number of different ways.

- Use it to test your own memory of Bible facts.

- Use it as an ice-breaker at get-togethers.

- Use it as a Bible pursuit game with a group of friends.

- Use it to find interesting facts and humor for sermons and speeches.

- Use it to pass the time while traveling with family and friends.

- Use it as a game with large groups— divide the people into teams and see who can answer the trivia question first.

As you read *Bible Trivia for Every Day,* I hope you have as much fun answering the questions as I did compiling them.

—Bob Phillips, Hume, California

Every word of God is pure;
He is a shield to those who
put their trust in Him.

Proverbs 30:5

Your word is a lamp to my feet
and a light to my path.

Psalm 119:105

Your word I have hidden in my heart,
that I might not sin against You.

Psalm 119:11

But Jesus answered him, saying,
"It is written, 'Man shall not live
by bread alone, but by
every word of God.'"

Luke 4:4

This book contains the mind of God, the state of man, the way of salvation, the doom of sinners, and the happiness of believers. Its doctrines are holy, its precepts are binding, its histories are true, and its decisions are immutable. Read it to be wise, believe it to be safe, and practice it to be holy. It contains light to direct you, food to support you, and comfort to cheer you. It is the traveler's map, the pilgrim's staff, the pilot's compass, the soldier's sword, and the Christian's charter. Here paradise is restored, heaven opened, and the gates of hell disclosed. Christ is its grand object, our good is its design, and the glory of God its end. It should fill the memory, rule the heart, and guide the feet. Read it slowly, frequently, and prayerfully. It is a mine of wealth, a paradise of glory, and a river of pleasure. It is given you in life, will be opened in the judgment, and will be remembered forever. It involves the high-est responsibility, will reward the greatest labor, and will condemn all who trifle with its sacred contents.

Anonymous

Bible Trivia
for the Beginner

1

How many men did King Nebuchadnezzar see walking around in a fiery furnace? *Four.*

DANIEL 3:25

✳ ✳ ✳

Who was the first one to see a rainbow in the sky? *Noah.*

GENESIS 9:11-17

✳ ✳ ✳

If you are carrying heavy burdens, who will take care of them? *Jesus.*

MATTHEW 11:28

What town is also called the "city of David"? *Bethlehem.*

LUKE 2:4

* * *

Jesus told His disciples to be as wise as what animal? *Serpents.*

MATTHEW 10:16

* * *

What did John the Baptist do with locusts and wild honey? *He ate them.*

MATTHEW 3:1-4

* * *

What did Daniel do three times a day at an open window? *He prayed.*

DANIEL 6:10

* * *

Who found grace in the eyes of the Lord?
Noah.

GENESIS 6:8

* * *

Jesus said He would make His disciples
into what? *Fishers of men.*

MATTHEW 4:19

* * *

Who were on the Mount of Transfigura-
tion with Jesus? *Peter, James, and John.*

MATTHEW 17:1

The Bible is God's chart for you to steer by,
to keep you from the bottom of the sea, and
to show you where the harbor is, and how to
reach it without running on rocks or bars.

Henry Ward Beecher

When wrath is directed toward you, what has the power to turn it away? *A soft answer.*

PROVERBS 15:1

* * *

Joseph, Mary, and Jesus lived in what city? *Nazareth.*

MATTHEW 2:23

* * *

In Cana of Galilee, when Jesus performed His miracle, what did He turn the water into? *Wine.*

JOHN 2:11

* * *

Where was Jesus arrested by soldiers? *The Garden of Gethsemane.*

MATTHEW 26:36-55

* * *

Who saw a burning bush that was not consumed by fire? *Moses.*

EXODUS 3:2-4

> Most people are bothered by those passages in Scripture which they cannot understand; but as for me, I always notice that the passages in Scripture which trouble me most are those that I do understand.
>
> Mark Twain

What is the longest psalm in the Bible? *Psalm 119.*

✳ ✳ ✳

How many books would it take to contain all the truth about Jesus? *More than all the books ever written.*

JOHN 21:25

✳ ✳ ✳

What did Jesus do to Bartimaeus, the blind man? *He restored his sight.*

MARK 10:46

✳ ✳ ✳

What did Aaron fashion from pure gold? *A calf.*

EXODUS 32:2-4

The word of God is quick, and powerful, and sharper than any twoedged sword, piercing even to the dividing asunder of soul and spirit, and of the joints and marrow, and is a discerner of the thoughts and intents of the heart.

Hebrews 4:12 (KJV)

What did Jesus do to disperse a crowd of men? *Wrote with His finger in the sand.*

JOHN 8:6

✳ ✳ ✳

After Jesus was born, what did the wise men from the East bring Him? *Gold, frankincense, and myrrh.*

MATTHEW 2:11

✳ ✳ ✳

The Bible states that we are to pray how often? *Without ceasing.*

1 THESSALONIANS 5:17

✳ ✳ ✳

What should be our goal in whatever we do in word or deed? *Bring glory to God.*

COLOSSIANS 3:17

✳ ✳ ✳

What can we overcome by doing good? *Evil.*

ROMANS 12:21

✳ ✳ ✳

How does the Bible describe God's regard for David? *He was a man after God's own heart.*

ACTS 13:22

This Book of the Law shall not depart from your mouth, but you shall meditate in it day and night, that you may observe to do according to all that is written in it. For then you will make your way prosperous, and then you will have good success.

Joshua 1:8

What did Pharaoh instruct his soldiers to do to all the male babies? *Cast them into the river.*

EXODUS 1:22

✳ ✳ ✳

How did Jesus say you can identify people? *By the way they act.*

MATTHEW 7:20

✳ ✳ ✳

What did Paul almost persuade King
Agrippa to do? *Become a Christian.*

ACTS 26:28

✳ ✳ ✳

How old was Joseph when he died?
He was 110 years old.

GENESIS 50:26

Blessed is the man who walks not in the
counsel of the ungodly, nor stands in the path
of sinners, nor sits in the seat of the scornful;
but his delight is in the law of the LORD, and
in His law he meditates day and night. He
shall be like a tree planted by the rivers of
water, that brings forth its fruit in its season,
whose leaf also shall not wither; and whatever he does shall prosper.

Psalm 1:1-3

How did Judas betray Jesus? *With a kiss.*

MATTHEW 26:47-49

❋ ❋ ❋

What occupation did Peter and many of the disciples have? *They were fishermen.*

MATTHEW 4:18

❋ ❋ ❋

What did Paul tell Timothy to take for his stomach problems? *A little wine.*

1 TIMOTHY 5:23

❋ ❋ ❋

Where did Ruth follow her mother-in-law to? *A foreign land.*

RUTH 1

❋ ❋ ❋

How many people did Jesus feed with the help of a little boy? *Five thousand.*

JOHN 6:9

* * *

The people sang a song to praise David when he killed how many people? *Ten thousand.*

1 SAMUEL 18:7-8

> Trust in the LORD with all your heart, and lean not on your own understanding; in all your ways acknowledge Him, and He shall direct your paths.
>
> Proverbs 3:5-6

After Judas betrayed Jesus, what did Judas do with the money? *He gave the money back to the priests.*

MATTHEW 27:3-5

* * *

Where did Jesus say no prophet is accepted? *In his own country.*

LUKE 4:24

✳ ✳ ✳

Where did Jesus often go to pray? *The Garden of Gethsemane.*

MATTHEW 26:36

A man has deprived himself of the best there is in the world who has deprived himself of this, a knowledge of the Bible. When you have read the Bible, you will know that it is the Word of God, because you will have found it the key to your own heart, your own happiness, and your own duty.

Woodrow Wilson

Who was the first person in the Bible to experience fear? *Adam.*

GENESIS 3:9-10

✳ ✳ ✳

Where are the great heroes of the Bible listed? *Hebrews 11.*

* * *

What did Paul do at a place called Mars Hill? *Preached a sermon.*

ACTS 17:22 (KJV)

* * *

Noah did not shut the door to the ark. Who did? *God.*

GENESIS 7:16

* * *

Where is Jesus' high priestly prayer found? *John 17.*

* * *

The Egyptians presumed that Sarah was what to Abraham? *His sister.*

GENESIS 12:19

* * *

Who was the first person in the Bible to take a nap? *Adam.*

GENESIS 2:20-21

Hold fast to the Bible as the sheet-anchor of your liberties; write its precepts in your hearts and practice them in your lives. To the influence of this book we are indebted for all the progress made in true civilization, and to this we must look as our guide in the future. Righteousness exalteth a nation; but sin is a reproach to any people.

Ulysses S. Grant

What is the first word in the Bible? *"In."*

GENESIS 1:1

✳ ✳ ✳

What is the last word in the Bible? *"Amen."*

REVELATION 22:21

✳ ✳ ✳

How often did the high priest enter the holy of holies? *Only once a year.*

LEVITICUS 16:34

* * *

When Jesus was under tremendous pressure, what was His sweat like? *Drops of blood.*

LUKE 22:44

* * *

Who was the treasurer of the disciples' money? *Judas Iscariot.*

JOHN 12:4-6

There is no book like the Bible for excellent learning, wisdom, and use.

Matthew Hale

Where in the Bible is the quotation, "God helps those who help themselves"? *It is not in the Bible.*

✳ ✳ ✳

What ruler asked Jesus if He was the King of the Jews? *Pilate.*

JOHN 18:33

✳ ✳ ✳

Who said, "I am a man of unclean lips"? *Isaiah.*

ISAIAH 6:5

✳ ✳ ✳

What chapter in the Bible is considered the love chapter? *First Corinthians 13.*

✳ ✳ ✳

Who or what told the first lie in the Bible?
The serpent.

GENESIS 3:4-5

Man shall not live by bread alone, but by
every word that proceedeth out of the
mouth of God.

Matthew 4:4 (KJV)

How many days did it take Nehemiah to
inspect the broken walls of Jerusalem?
Three days.

NEHEMIAH 2:11-13

✳ ✳ ✳

On what island did John write the book of
Revelation? *Patmos.*

REVELATION 1:9-11

✳ ✳ ✳

Who was the first person to enter Jesus' empty tomb? *Peter.*

JOHN 20:4-6

✳ ✳ ✳

What did Lydia sell? *Purple cloth.*

ACTS 16:14

✳ ✳ ✳

How many times is the word "Bible" found in the Bible? *None.*

> There never was found, in any age of the world, either religion or law that did so highly exalt the public good as the Bible.
>
> **Francis Bacon**

Which New Testament verse is one of the most memorized Bible verses? *John 3:16.*

✳ ✳ ✳

In what book of the Bible do you find the phrase, "cleanliness is next to godliness"? *It is not in the Bible.*

✳ ✳ ✳

Which disciple touched the wounds of Jesus? *Thomas.*

JOHN 20:25-27

✳ ✳ ✳

When Mary and Martha's brother died, what dramatic thing happened? *He was raised from the dead.*

JOHN 11:1-2

✳ ✳ ✳

Who bought a boat ticket in the city of Joppa? *Jonah.*

JONAH 1:3

✳ ✳ ✳

If we abide by the principles taught in the
Bible, our country will go on prospering
and to prosper; but if we and our posterity
neglect its instructions and authority, no man
can tell how sudden a catastrophe may over-
whelm us and bury our glory in profound
obscurity.

Daniel Webster

What was the apostle Paul's occupation?
He was a tentmaker.

ACTS 18:1-3

✳ ✳ ✳

How much older than Jesus was John the
Baptist? *Six months.*

LUKE 1:24-27,36,56,57

✳ ✳ ✳

Who said, "There's nothing new under the
sun"? *King Solomon.*

ECCLESIASTES 1:9

✳ ✳ ✳

What is the beginning of knowledge?
The fear of the Lord.

PROVERBS 1:7

* * *

Who said that no one is able to tame the
tongue? *James, the brother of Jesus.*

JAMES 3:7

It is impossible to enslave mentally or socially
a Bible-reading people. The principles of the
Bible are the groundwork of human freedom.

Horace Greeley

Who did Jesus rebuke by saying, "Get
thee behind me, Satan"? *Peter.*

MATTHEW 16:23 (KJV)

* * *

Where was the prophet Jonah at when he prayed for deliverance? *He was inside a large fish.*

JONAH 2:1

* * *

What special food did God prepare for the Israelites? *Manna.*

EXODUS 16:14-15

> The Bible is worth all the other books which have ever been printed.
>
> **Patrick Henry**

Who was given a coat made from many colors? *Joseph.*

GENESIS 37:3

* * *

Whose wife disobeyed God and was
turned into a pillar of salt? *Lot.*

GENESIS 19:15-26

* * *

What did the prodigal son eat when he
went to a foreign country? *Pig's food.*

LUKE 15:11-16

* * *

What has God prepared for those who
believe? *A house with many mansions.*

JOHN 14:2

* * *

The Old Testament contains how many
different books? *Thirty-nine.*

* * *

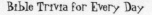

> The Bible is a book in comparison with which
> all others in my eyes are of minor impor-
> tance; and which in all my perplexities and
> distresses has never failed to give me light
> and strength.
>
> **Robert E. Lee**

Who have some people unknowingly
entertained? *Angels.*

HEBREWS 13:2

✻ ✻ ✻

What did Jesus say you should do if your
right eye offends you? *Pluck it out.*

MATTHEW 5:29 (KJV)

✻ ✻ ✻

Who wanted to know how a man could be
born when he was old? *Nicodemus.*

JOHN 3:4

✻ ✻ ✻

A person was once healed by simply touching what part of Jesus' clothes? *The hem of His robe.*

MARK 5:30

It was the Lord who put into my mind (I could feel His hand upon me) the fact that it would be possible to sail from here to the Indies. All who heard of my project rejected it with laughter, ridiculing me. There is no question that the inspiration was from the Holy Spirit, because He comforted me with rays of marvelous inspiration from the Holy Scriptures.

Christopher Columbus

What is the shortest verse in the New Testament? *"Jesus wept."*

JOHN 11:35

✳ ✳ ✳

What person does the Bible suggest had great patience? *Job.*

JOB 1–42

* * *

Abel was a "keeper of sheep." What was Cain? *A farmer—"a tiller of the ground."*

GENESIS 4:2

* * *

What modern phrase do we get from one of Jesus' disciples? *"Doubting Thomas."*

JOHN 20:24-29

* * *

What does God know about the hairs on your head? *The number of them.*

MATTHEW 10:30

* * *

How many gallons of water did Jesus turn into wine at a wedding feast? *More than 100 gallons.*

JOHN 2:1-11

The meaning of the Bible must be known and understood if it is to make a difference in our lives, and I urge all Americans to read and study the Scriptures. The rewards of such efforts will help preserve our heritage of freedom and signal the message of liberty to people in all lands.

Ronald Reagan

What did Adam and Eve sew together to make clothes for themselves? *Leaves.*

GENESIS 3:7

✳ ✳ ✳

Gideon conquered a very large army with how many men? *Only 300.*

JUDGES 7:15-16

* * *

What did Aaron take from both men and women? *Golden earrings.*

EXODUS 32:2-4

* * *

What came out of Jesus when the Romans pierced His side? *Blood and water.*

JOHN 19:34

* * *

What happened to Ananias and his wife when they lied to God? *They both died.*

ACTS 5:1-11

* * *

I gleaned more practical psychology and psychiatry from the Bible, than from all other books.

George W. Crane

Judas agreed to betray Jesus for how many pieces of silver? *Thirty.*

MATTHEW 26:14-15

❋ ❋ ❋

What will be given to you if you ask God and believe He will answer? *Wisdom.*

JAMES 1:5-6

❋ ❋ ❋

What is the beast's identification number from the book of Revelation? *It is 666.*

REVELATION 13:18

❋ ❋ ❋

What was the name of the angel who
spoke to Mary? *Gabriel.*

LUKE 2:26-27

So great is my veneration of the Bible that
the earlier my children begin to read it, the
more confident will be my hope that they
will prove useful citizens of their country and
respectable members of society.

John Quincy Adams

Bible Trivia for the Novice

2

Who said he would exalt his throne above God's throne? *Lucifer, also known as Satan.*

ISAIAH 14:13

* * *

What book of the Bible talks about 100-pound hailstones? *Revelation.*

REVELATION 16:21

* * *

Who had a spear with an iron head weighing 600 shekels? *Goliath.*

1 SAMUEL 17:4,7

Did Adam and Eve eat an apple?
No. It was a fruit of some kind.

GENESIS 3

* * *

Which disciple's second sermon resulted
in about 5000 people coming to Christ?
Peter.

ACTS 4:4

> Your words were found, and I ate them, and
> Your word was to me the joy and rejoicing
> of my heart; for I am called by Your name, O
> LORD God of hosts.
>
> Jeremiah 15:16

How many years are but one day to God?
One thousand.

PSALM 90:4

Who took care of Jesus' mother after He died? *John the disciple.*

JOHN 19:26-27

✳ ✳ ✳

What king had a troubled spirit that could only be soothed by music? *King Saul.*

1 SAMUEL 16:14-23

✳ ✳ ✳

What is the shortest prayer in the Bible? *"Lord, save me."*

MATTHEW 14:30

But these are written that you may believe that Jesus is the Christ, the Son of God, and that believing you may have life in His name.

John 20:31

What is more desirable than great riches?
A good name.

PROVERBS 22:1

* * *

How many people did Jesus appear to
after His resurrection? *More than 500.*

1 CORINTHIANS 15:6

* * *

What did Moses, Elijah, and Jesus each
do for 40 days? *Fasted.*

EXODUS 34:27-28; 1 KINGS 19:2,8;
MATTHEW 4:2

* * *

What one thing did the rich man in hell
desire? *Water.*

LUKE 16:22-24

* * *

What punishment did God give Eve?
Pain during childbirth.

GENESIS 3:16

Our faith is not dependent upon human
knowledge and scientific advance, but upon
the unmistakable message of the Word of
God.

Billy Graham

After Mary washed Jesus' feet with per-
fume, with what did she wipe them?
Her hair.

JOHN 12:3-5

✳ ✳ ✳

What does the Bible suggest we should
not eat too much of? *Honey.*

PROVERBS 25:16

✳ ✳ ✳

What did the Israelite men not do for one year after being married? *Go to war.*

DEUTERONOMY 24:5

✳ ✳ ✳

Which angel fights with the dragon? *Michael.*

REVELATION 12:7

America was born a Christian nation. America was born to exemplify that devotion to the elements of righteousness which are derived from the revelations of Holy Scriptures.

Woodrow Wilson

Which Old Testament prophet was described as being a bald-headed man? *Elisha.*

2 KINGS 2:23

✳ ✳ ✳

Which Old Testament prophet was very
hairy and wore a leather belt? *Elijah.*

2 KINGS 1:8

✳ ✳ ✳

What did King David arrange to have
done to Uriah? *Have him murdered.*

2 SAMUEL 11:2-17

The Scriptures teach us the best way of living,
the noblest way of suffering, and the most
comfortable way of dying.

Flavel

Who inherited Elijah's mantle? *Elisha.*

2 KINGS 2:12-13

✳ ✳ ✳

How long did Jacob work to earn the hand of his wife? *Seven years.*

GENESIS 29:20

> The best evidence of the Bible's being the word of God is to be found between its covers. It proves itself.
>
> Charles Hodge

What did Peter do to Malchus, the high priest's servant? *Cut off his right ear.*

JOHN 18:10

* * *

With what did David cut off Goliath's head? *The giant's own sword.*

1 SAMUEL 17:50-51

* * *

Who came from afar to listen to Solomon's wisdom? *The Queen of Sheba.*

1 KINGS 10:1-13

> Finally, brethren, whatever things are true, whatever things are noble, whatever things are just, whatever things are pure, whatever things are lovely, whatever things are of good report, if there is any virtue and if there is anything praiseworthy—meditate on these things.
>
> Philippians 4:8

What did the Egyptians find in their beds and in their ovens? *Frogs.*

EXODUS 8:3,6

❊ ❊ ❊

What did Solomon suggest to cut in half in order to settle an argument? *A baby.*

1 KINGS 3:15,25

❊ ❊ ❊

While in Damascus, for how many days
was Saul (Paul) blinded? *Three.*

ACTS 9:8-9

* * *

Methuselah, the oldest man in the Bible,
died when he was how many years old?
He was 969 years old.

GENESIS 5:27

* * *

Who were called the "Sons of Thunder"?
James and John.

MARK 3:17

* * *

Who was the first woman judge of Israel?
Deborah.

JUDGES 4:4

* * *

What did Paul use as a means of escape
in Damascus? *A basket.*

ACTS 9:23-25

✳ ✳ ✳

Dogs devoured which Old Testament
queen? *Queen Jezebel.*

1 KINGS 16:30-31; 2 KINGS 9:36

It is a belief in the Bible, the fruits of deep
meditation, which has served me as the guide
of my moral and literary life. I have found it a
capital safely invested, and richly productive
of interest.

Johanne Goethe

While in the wilderness, the children of
Israel ate manna for how many years?
Forty.

EXODUS 16:35

✳ ✳ ✳

How many years did it take Noah to build the ark? *One hundred twenty.*

GENESIS 6:3

* * *

Where were the Ten Commandments, Aaron's rod, and manna kept? *In the ark of the covenant.*

HEBREWS 9:4

* * *

What was the color of Esau's complexion? *Red.*

GENESIS 25:25

* * *

As the soldiers taunted Jesus, they placed a robe on Him. What color was the robe? *Purple.*

JOHN 19:2

* * *

How many hours did Jesus hang on the cross before He died? *Six.*

MARK 15:25,34-37

* * *

What did the mother of James and John request of Jesus? *That her sons sit on either side of Him in His kingdom.*

MATTHEW 10:2; 20:20-24

* * *

What name did Jacob later go by? *Israel.*

GENESIS 32:28

* * *

Why did Jonah become angry with the people of Nineveh? *They repented.*

JONAH 3:1-10; 4:1

* * *

Who had a wrestling match with God and won? *Jacob.*

GENESIS 32:24-30

* * *

How many times was the apostle Paul shipwrecked? *Three.*

2 CORINTHIANS 11:25

* * *

Who had 700 wives and 300 concubines? *King Solomon.*

1 KINGS 11:1,3

* * *

Who prayed the longest prayer recorded in the Bible and where is it written? *Jesus in John 17.*

* * *

What did Jesus do with five loaves of bread and two fishes? *He fed five thousand people.*

MATTHEW 14:17-21

These things I have written to you who believe in the name of the Son of God, that you may know that you have eternal life, and that you may continue to believe in the name of the Son of God.

I John 5:13

What name did Matthew use before Jesus renamed him? *Levi.*

MARK 2:14; LUKE 5:27; MATTHEW 9:9

✳ ✳ ✳

Who was bitten by a poisonous snake and yet lived? *The apostle Paul.*

ACTS 28:3-5

✳ ✳ ✳

How many times was Peter told to
forgive someone who sins against him?
Seventy times seven—490.

MATTHEW 18:21-22

* * *

Delilah hounded Samson until he told her
what? *The source of his strength.*

JUDGES 16:6

* * *

What can pride lead to? *Destruction.*

PROVERBS 16:18

* * *

What was the name of Peter's brother?
Andrew.

MATTHEW 10:2

* * *

Joseph, Mary, and Jesus had to flee to what country? *Egypt.*

MATTHEW 2:13

* * *

Who came from the East to visit the young Jesus? *Wise men.*

MATTHEW 2:1

* * *

Who was considered the wisest man? *King Solomon.*

1 KINGS 3:11-12

* * *

How many separate books are there in the New Testament? *Twenty-seven.*

* * *

Who directs the steps of good men? *God.*

PSALM 37:23

* * *

Who was called "the good shepherd"?
Jesus.

JOHN 10:11

* * *

Living a life of sin is death, but those who
live for God get what? *Eternal life.*

ROMANS 6:23

* * *

Who was called a murderer and liar?
Satan.

JOHN 8:44

* * *

What was the name of Abraham's wife?
Sarah.

GENESIS 17:15

* * *

What did God curse in the Garden of Eden? *The serpent.*

GENESIS 3:14

✳ ✳ ✳

What was David before he became king? *A shepherd.*

1 SAMUEL 16:11-13

✳ ✳ ✳

What is greater than having faith and hope? *Having love.*

1 CORINTHIANS 13:13

✳ ✳ ✳

What did Jesus' earthly father do for a living? *He was a carpenter.*

MATTHEW 13:55

✳ ✳ ✳

For those who believe, what does the Lord
become? *A shield.*

PSALM 28:7

* * *

How is the greatest love displayed?
Dying for another.

JOHN 15:13

* * *

Who was called the "light of the world"?
Jesus.

JOHN 8:12

* * *

How did Jesus still stormy waters?
He spoke a word.

MARK 4:37-39

3

Bible Trivia
for the Rookie

Jesus had two brothers who wrote books
in the Bible. What were their names?
James and Jude.

MATTHEW 13:55

* * *

Why did Miriam and Aaron become upset
with Moses? *He married an Ethiopian.*

NUMBERS 12:1

* * *

How many pairs of each clean
animal did Noah take onto the ark?
Seven.

GENESIS 7:2

* * *

Samson told a riddle to the Philistines
about what animal? *A lion.*

JUDGES 14:12-14

* * *

What did Solomon say can bite like a
serpent? *Wine.*

PROVERBS 23:31-32

* * *

What type of bird did Noah send out from
the ark three different times? *A dove.*

GENESIS 8:8-12

* * *

What did the Israelites experience for 430 years? *Bondage as slaves.*

EXODUS 12:40

* * *

Who was swept away in a whirlwind? *Elijah.*

2 KINGS 2:11

* * *

What object did Jacob dream about that reached up to heaven? *A ladder.*

GENESIS 28:10-12

* * *

Who was the first of the disciples to be murdered? *James.*

ACTS 12:1-2

* * *

All that I am I owe to Jesus Christ, revealed
to me in His divine Book.

David Livingstone

What did King Solomon own that were
made of pure gold? *Dishes.*

1 KINGS 10:21

* * *

What is another name for the city of
Jericho? *"The city of palm trees."*

DEUTERONOMY 34:3

* * *

Who was the first New Testament
martyr? *John the Baptist.*

MATTHEW 14:10

* * *

What had five porches around it? *The pool of Bethesda.*

JOHN 5:2

* * *

Ezekiel preached in a valley full of what? *Dead men's bones.*

EZEKIEL 37:1-14

> The Bible is one of the greatest blessings bestowed by God on the children of men—It has God for its author; salvation for its end, and truth without any mixture for its matter—It is all pure, all sincere; nothing too much; nothing wanting.
>
> John Locke

What did Elisha use to purify drinking water? *Salt.*

2 KINGS 2:20-22

* * *

How old was Noah when it began to rain on him and his family? *He was 600 years old.*

GENESIS 7:11

* * *

When Elisha raised a dead boy to life, how many times did the boy sneeze? *Seven.*

2 KINGS 4:32-35

* * *

What did Elijah do with a poor widow's last meal? *He ate it.*

1 KINGS 17:10-15

* * *

Who came to rescue Lot from destruction? *Two angels.*

GENESIS 19:1

* * *

What relation was Mordecai to Queen
Esther? *He was her cousin.*

ESTHER 2:5-7

✳ ✳ ✳

Why were Ishmael and his mother sent
out to the desert? *To die.*

GENESIS 16:15; 21:14

✳ ✳ ✳

What request regarding John the Baptist
did Herodias' daughter make?
She asked for his head.

MATTHEW 14:6-11

✳ ✳ ✳

With what did the Gibeonites fool Joshua?
Dry and moldy bread.

JOSHUA 9:3-5,12

✳ ✳ ✳

I thoroughly believe in a university education for both men and women; but I believe a knowledge of the Bible without a college course is more valuable than a college course without the Bible.

William Lyons Phelps

With what did Noah build the ark?
Gopher wood.

GENESIS 6:14

* * *

When Abraham asked God to spare a city, how many upright people needed to live in it? *Ten.*

GENESIS 18:32

* * *

What did Hagar do with her young son?
She cast him into the bushes.

GENESIS 21:14-15

Where did Jochebed hide Moses to save his life? *In the bulrushes.*

EXODUS 2:3; 6:20

* * *

Jesus fed 4000 people with how many loaves of bread? *Seven.*

MATTHEW 15:36-38

* * *

What book was the Ethiopian eunuch reading when Philip met him? *The book of Isaiah.*

ACTS 8:27-30

I don't think you can possibly grow up in an education in which the exposition of the life and the meaning of life of Jesus is central, and not say that the New Testament is the most important book in your life, however much or little you may have in fact lived by it. It's the most powerful single volume you encounter.

McGeorge Bundy

The soldiers divided Jesus' garments into how many parts? *Four.*

JOHN 19:23

* * *

When Esau was born, Jacob was holding onto what part of Esau's body? *His heel.*

GENESIS 25:23-26

* * *

What resulted from Jacob wrestling with God? *Jacob became lame.*

GENESIS 32:24-31

* * *

When Aaron cast down his rod, what did it turn into? *A serpent.*

EXODUS 7:10

* * *

What relation was Lois to Timothy?
She was his grandmother.

2 TIMOTHY 1:5

All Scripture is given by inspiration of God, and is profitable for doctrine, for reproof, for correction, for instruction in righteousness, that the man of God may be complete, thoroughly equipped for every good work.

2 Timothy 3:16-17

God loved Jacob. How did God regard Jacob's brother Esau? *He hated him.*

ROMANS 9:13

✳ ✳ ✳

Which Old Testament prophet foretold the virgin birth of Christ? *Isaiah.*

ISAIAH 7:14

✳ ✳ ✳

Where did Rahab the prostitute hide two of Joshua's spies? *On her roof.*

JOSHUA 2:1-6

✳ ✳ ✳

To what does the Bible liken a life of sin? *To a dog and a pig.*

2 PETER 2:20-22

✳ ✳ ✳

What was the name of the disciple Priscilla and Aquila helped train? *Apollos.*

ACTS 18:24-26

I have made it a practice for several years to read the Bible through in the course of every year.

John Quincy Adams

What happened to Moses' hand when he stuck it inside his cloak? *It became leprous.*

EXODUS 4:6

* * *

When Satan smote Job with sores, how much of his body did they cover? *From his feet to the top of his head.*

JOB 2:7

* * *

Haman was hung on a gallows that was how high? *About 70 feet.*

ESTHER 7:9-10

* * *

What was the first bird Noah sent out from the ark to find dry land? *A raven.*

GENESIS 8:6-7

* * *

What was the name of King David's first wife? *Michal*.

1 SAMUEL 18:27

> The book to read is not the one which thinks for you, but the one which makes you think. No book in the world equals the Bible for that.
>
> James McCosh

What did Paul do to the sorcerer named Elymas? *He struck him blind*.

ACTS 13:6-12

* * *

What happened when, in the middle of a battle, Aaron and Hur held up Moses' hands? *The Israelites were victorious*.

EXODUS 17:11-13

* * *

What was the name of Moses' wife?
Zipporah.

EXODUS 2:21

❋ ❋ ❋

To what does the Bible compare a
beautiful woman who lacks discretion?
A jewel of gold in a swine's snout.

PROVERBS 11:22

❋ ❋ ❋

What does the Bible say it is not good to
do early in the morning? *To loudly bless
your neighbor.*

PROVERBS 27:14

No man ever did, nor ever will become truly
eloquent, without being a constant reader of
the Bible, and admirer of the purity and sub-
limity of its language.

Fisher Ames

King Og's large bed was made of what?
Iron.

                              DEUTERONOMY 3:11

* * *

What did a woman do because she was
scorned by Joseph? *She faked a rape.*

                              GENESIS 39:10-15

* * *

What happened to the apostle Paul in the
city of Lystra? *He was stoned.*

                              ACTS 14:8-19

* * *

How many people died when Abimelech
set fire to a tower? *One thousand.*

                              JUDGES 9:47-49

* * *

How long did Noah live after the flood?
For 350 years.

GENESIS 9:28

> I use the Scriptures, not as an arsenal to be
> resorted to only for arms and weapons, but
> as a matchless temple, where I delight to be,
> to contemplate the beauty, the symmetry,
> and the magnificence of the structure, and to
> increase my awe and excite my devotion to
> the Deity there preached and adored.
>
> **Boyle**

What part of the holy city of God will be
made of pearls? *The gates.*

REVELATION 21:21

✳ ✳ ✳

David took Saul's spear and water jug, but
did not do what to Saul? *Kill him.*

1 SAMUEL 26:7-12

✳ ✳ ✳

What was the name of Elisha's servant?
Gehazi.

2 KINGS 4:25

* * *

What was the color of the manna the
Israelites ate? *White.*

EXODUS 16:31

I speak as a man of the world to men of the
world; and I say to you, search the Scriptures! The Bible is the book of all others, to
be read at all ages, and in all conditions of
human life; not to be read once or twice or
thrice through, and then laid aside, but to be
read in small portions of one or two chapters every day, and never to be intermitted,
unless by some overruling necessity.

John Quincy Adams

What person was the New Testament book Third John written to? *Gaius.*

3 JOHN 1

* * *

What piece of clothing did Job compare to acting justly? *A turban.*

JOB 29:14

* * *

What did Jael hammer through a man's head? *A tent peg.*

JUDGES 4:9-24

* * *

Who was the first person in the Bible to go to prison? *Joseph.*

GENESIS 39:20

* * *

Who gives names to the stars? *God.*

PSALM 147:4

* * *

Because of a vow, what did Paul do to his hair? *Cut it off.*

ACTS 18:18

* * *

To whom did Jesus say, "You gave me no kiss"? *Simon.*

LUKE 7:44-45

4

Bible Trivia for the Scholar

What did God tell Hosea to do? *Marry a prostitute.*

HOSEA 1:2

* * *

After Cain killed Abel, where did Cain sleep? *In the land of Nod.*

GENESIS 4:16

* * *

Who was considered a mighty hunter before the Lord? *Nimrod.*

GENESIS 10:8-9

Elijah was also known by what name?
The Tishbite.

1 KINGS 17:1

＊ ＊ ＊

Where did David ask God to put his
tears? *Into a bottle.*

PSALM 56:8

In regard to this Great Book, I have but to
say, it is the best gift God has given to man.
All the good the Savior gave to the world
was communicated through this book. But
for it we could not know right from wrong.

Abraham Lincoln

What is the meaning of the word
"Ichabod"? *The glory has departed.*

1 SAMUEL 4:21

＊ ＊ ＊

What was the name of the runaway slave who went back to his master? *Onesimus.*

PHILEMON 10–12

✻ ✻ ✻

Who accidentally hanged himself in a tree? *Absalom.*

2 SAMUEL 18:9

✻ ✻ ✻

What king saw a mysterious hand writing on the wall? *King Belshazzar.*

DANIEL 5:5

✻ ✻ ✻

Who slept at the feet of Boaz before she was married to him? *Ruth.*

RUTH 3:7-9; 4:10

✻ ✻ ✻

Why did Elisha curse 42 children?
They called him baldheaded.

2 KINGS 2:23-24

* * *

What happened to the 42 children Elisha
cursed? *They were killed by two bears.*

2 KINGS 2:23-24

* * *

Who was known for driving his chariot in
a furious manner? *Jehu.*

2 KINGS 9:20

* * *

Why was it difficult to kill King Eglon
with a knife? *He was a very fat man.*

JUDGES 3:22

* * *

What was touched to the lips of Isaiah?
A live coal from a fire.

ISAIAH 6:6-7

> So great is my veneration for the Bible, that
> the earlier my children begin to read it the
> more confident will be my hopes that they
> will prove useful citizens to their country and
> respectable members of society.
>
> John Quincy Adams

Where was Jesus at when the three wise
men visited Him? *In a house in Bethlehem.*

MATTHEW 2:1-2,11

✳ ✳ ✳

Who changed dust into lice? *Aaron.*

EXODUS 8:17

✳ ✳ ✳

What book of the Bible does not contain
the name of God? *The book of Esther.*

* * *

Who made a lost ax head float on water?
Elisha.

2 KINGS 6:5-7

* * *

Why did King Ahab pout on his bed?
Because he could not buy land.

1 KINGS 21:2-4

The Bible is not an end in itself, but a means
to bring men to an intimate and satisfying
knowledge of God, that they may enter into
Him, that they may delight in His Presence,
may taste and know the inner sweetness of
the very God Himself in the core and center
of their hearts.

A.W. Tozer

What is the name of the first musician in the Bible? *Jubal.*

GENESIS 4:21

* * *

Who had 15 years added to his life? *Hezekiah.*

ISAIAH 38:5

* * *

How many pounds of myrrh and aloes did Nicodemus put on the body of Jesus? *One hundred.*

JOHN 19:39

* * *

How many times did Elijah tell his servant to look for a cloud? *Seven.*

1 KINGS 18:42-44

* * *

How many men were sent to capture
Samson? *Three thousand.*

JUDGES 15:11

* * *

How many men in the Bible were named
Judas? *Six.*

MATTHEW 10:4; 13:55; LUKE 6:16;
ACTS 5:37; 9:11; 15:22

> It is Christ Himself, not the Bible, who is the
> true word of God. The Bible, read in the
> right spirit, and with the guidance of good
> teachers, will bring us to Him.
>
> C.S. Lewis

The first mention of a "lunatic" is found in
what book? *Matthew.*

MATTHEW 4:24 (KJV)

* * *

What is manna said to have tasted like?
Wafers with honey.

EXODUS 16:31; NUMBERS 11:8

* * *

Nebuchadnezzar had fingernails that
looked like what? *Bird claws.*

DANIEL 4:33-34

* * *

Elijah could run faster than what?
A chariot.

1 KINGS 18:45-46

> We fail in our duty to study God's Word not
> so much because it is difficult to understand,
> not so much because it is dull and boring, but
> because it is work. Our problem is not a lack
> of intelligence or a lack of passion. Our prob-
> lem is that we are lazy.
>
> **R.C. Sproul**

How many soldiers guarded Peter while he was in prison? *Sixteen*.

ACTS 12:3-4

* * *

Who was the fourth oldest man in the Bible? *Adam*.

GENESIS 5:5,20,27; 9:29

To get the full flavor of an herb, it must be pressed between the fingers, so it is the same with the Scriptures; the more familiar they become, the more they reveal their hidden treasures and yield their indescribable riches.

John Chrysostom

Who does the Bible call the most humble man? *Moses*.

NUMBERS 12:3

* * *

Who had his carriage upholstered in purple? *Solomon.*

SONG OF SOLOMON 3:9-10

* * *

What happened to Job's skin when he became ill? *It turned black.*

JOB 30:30

* * *

Who is the woman most mentioned in the Bible? *Sarah. She is mentioned 60 times.*

* * *

How was Ezekiel lifted between heaven and earth? *By his hair.*

EZEKIEL 8:3

* * *

What did Amos call the sinful women of
Israel? *Cows of Bashan.*

AMOS 4:1

> The Bible is a corridor between two eterni-
> ties down which walks the Christ of God; His
> invisible steps echo through the Old Testa-
> ment, but we meet Him face to face in the
> throne room of the New; and it is through
> that Christ alone, crucified for me, that I have
> found forgiveness for sins and life eternal.
> The Old Testament is summed up in the
> word Christ; the New Testament is summed
> up in the word Jesus; and the summary of
> the whole Bible is that Jesus is the Christ.
>
> **Bishop Pollock**

How old was Adam when he died?
He was 930.

GENESIS 5:5

✳ ✳ ✳

How old was Enoch when God took him to heaven? *He was 365.*

GENESIS 5:23-24

❊ ❊ ❊

What was Ephraim called?
A half-baked pancake.

HOSEA 7:8

❊ ❊ ❊

What happend to Jeremiah when he was put into prison? *He sank in the mire.*

JEREMIAH 38:5-6

❊ ❊ ❊

Whose sons were named Muppim, Huppim, and Ard? *Benjamin's.*

GENESIS 46:21

❊ ❊ ❊

Whose head was cut off and thrown over a wall? *Sheba's.*

2 SAMUEL 20:14-22

* * *

What was the name of Paul's secretary who wrote Romans? *Tertius.*

ROMANS 16:22

What we really need, after all, is not to defend the Bible but to understand it.

Millar Burrows

What did Aaron's rod yield after it blossomed? *Almonds.*

NUMBERS 17:8

* * *

How fast could David's mighty men run?
As fast as gazelles.

1 CHRONICLES 12:8

* * *

How many men from the tribe of Benjamin could sling rocks with either hand?
Seven hundred.

JUDGES 20:15-16

* * *

What happened to Eutychus during Paul's sermon? *He fell asleep and fell out of a window.*

ACTS 20:9

* * *

What is the shortest verse in the Old Testament? *Eber, Peleg, Rue.*

1 CHRONICLES 1:25

* * *

The Zamzummims were a race of what kind of people? *Giants.*

DEUTERONOMY 2:20

✳ ✳ ✳

What is the longest word in the Bible? *Mahershalalhashbaz.*

ISAIAH 8:1,3

✳ ✳ ✳

Job talked about washing steps with what? *Butter.*

JOB 29:1,6

Nobody ever outgrows Scripture; the book widens and deepens with our years.

Charles Haddon Spurgeon

What was the name of Jeremiah's secretary? *Baruch.*

JEREMIAH 36:10,17-18

✳ ✳ ✳

Which dressmaker was raised from the dead? *Dorcas.*

ACTS 9:36-40

All Scripture is given by inspiration of God, and is profitable for doctrine, for reproof, for correction, for instruction in righteousness: That the man of God may be perfect, thoroughly furnished unto all good works.

2 Timothy 3:16,17 (KJV)

Abimelech, the son of Gideon, killed how many of his brothers? *Sixty-nine.*

JUDGES 9:4-5

✳ ✳ ✳

What condition did Mephibosheth suffer after his nurse dropped him when he was a baby? *He became crippled for life.*

2 SAMUEL 4:4

* * *

What did Benaiah do on a snowy day? *He killed a lion in a pit.*

1 CHRONICLES 11:22

* * *

When Ezekiel ate a book, he thought it was as sweet as what? *Honey.*

EZEKIEL 2:9; 3:3

* * *

Who asked, "Is there any taste in the white of an egg?" *Job.*

JOB 6:6

* * *

At only two verses long, what psalm is the shortest chapter in the Bible? *Psalm 117.*

✳ ✳ ✳

How many men did Adino the Eznite kill with a spear? *Eight hundred.*

2 SAMUEL 23:8

It is rightly impossible to govern the world without God and the Bible.

George Washington

How many men in the Bible were named Dodo? *Three.*

JUDGES 10:1; 2 SAMUEL 23:9,24

✳ ✳ ✳

What did Ezra do because of his interracial marriage? *He pulled out his hair.*

EZRA 9:1-3

✳ ✳ ✳

Who was the first bigamist mentioned in
the Bible? *Lamech.*

GENESIS 4:19

* * *

How many men did Shamgar kill with an
ox goad? *Six hundred.*

JUDGES 3:31

* * *

What animal does the Bible mention as
wearing necklaces? *Camels.*

JUDGES 8:21,26

* * *

Forty-two thousand men were killed for
mispronouncing what word? *"Shibboleth."*

JUDGES 12:5-6

* * *

Search the scriptures; for in them ye think
ye have eternal life; and they are they which
testify of me.

John 5:39 (KJV)

During a great famine, what did one
woman do when she became desperately
hungry? *She ate her own son.*

2 KINGS 6:25-29

✳ ✳ ✳

Who killed a seven-and-a-half-foot-tall
giant? *Benaiah.*

1 CHRONICLES 11:22-23

✳ ✳ ✳

How many men were killed when a wall
fell on them? *Twenty-seven thousand.*

1 KINGS 20:30

✳ ✳ ✳

The whole inspiration of our civilization springs from the teachings of Christ and the lessons of the prophets. To read the Bible for these fundamentals is a necessity of American life.

Herbert Hoover

Jonathan killed a giant who had how many fingers and toes? *Twelve fingers and twelve toes.*

2 SAMUEL 21:20-21

✳ ✳ ✳

What did Zimri do to his own palace? *He set fire to it and died in the flames.*

1 KINGS 16:18

✳ ✳ ✳

How many locks of hair did Delilah have
a man cut from the head of Samson?
Seven.

JUDGES 16:18-19

* * *

What city was also known as Jebus and
Salem? *Jerusalem.*

JUDGES 19:10; PSALM 76:2

* * *

What is the longest verse in the Bible?
Esther 8:7.

* * *

Ahasuerus had women perfumed for how
long before they came to him? *A year.*

ESTHER 2:12

* * *

Repentance is a hearty sorrow for our past misdeeds, and is a sincere resolution and endeavor, to the utmost of our power, to conform all our actions to the law of God. It does not consist in one single act of sorrow, but in doing works meet for repentance; in a sincere obedience to the law of Christ for the remainder of our lives.

John Locke

What book of the Bible talks about "wimples and the crisping pins"? *Isaiah.*

✳ ✳ ✳

Ezekiel was told to lie on his right side for how many days? *Forty.*

EZEKIEL 4:6

✳ ✳ ✳

Ben-Hadad was smothered to death by what? *A wet cloth.*

2 KINGS 8:14-15

* * *

How did God destroy the kings who attacked Gibeon? *Hailstones.*

JOSHUA 10:5,11

* * *

How many chapters are there in the Bible? *There are 1189.*

* * *

What was the name of the giant Goliath's brother? *Lahmi.*

1 CHRONICLES 20:5

* * *

Who is mentioned in the Bible as having an incurable bowel disease? *Jehoram.*

2 CHRONICLES 21:18

The Bible is a window in this prison-world, through which we may look into eternity.

Timothy Dwight

How many suicides are mentioned in the Bible? *Seven.*

✳ ✳ ✳

How often did Hannah make a coat for her son Samuel? *Every year.*

1 SAMUEL 1:20; 2:18-19

✳ ✳ ✳

In order to save his own life, what did David pretend to be? *Crazy.*

1 SAMUEL 21:12-15

✳ ✳ ✳

What was Nebuchadnezzar's father's name? *Belshazzar.*

DANIEL 5:2

✳ ✳ ✳

Which angel debated with the devil? *Michael.*

JUDE 1:9

✳ ✳ ✳

How many days was Noah in the ark before it started to rain? *Seven days.*

GENESIS 7:1,4

✳ ✳ ✳

What type of bird fed the prophet Elijah when he was in the wilderness? *Ravens.*

1 KINGS 17:1-6

✳ ✳ ✳

Who was saved by a scarlet cord?
Rahab and her family.

JOSHUA 2:1,18

* * *

What was unique about the man who
killed King Eglon? *He was left-handed.*

JUDGES 3:15-25

* * *

How many books of the Bible were written
to Theophilus? *Two.*

LUKE 1:3; ACTS 1:1

* * *

How many husbands had the woman from
Samaria had? *Five.*

JOHN 4:7,17-18

* * *

What other name did King Solomon have?
Jedidiah.

2 SAMUEL 12:24-25

❊ ❊ ❊

How often did Absalom cut his hair?
Only once a year.

2 SAMUEL 14:25-26

❊ ❊ ❊

What did Balaam's donkey do?
It spoke to him.

NUMBERS 22:28

❊ ❊ ❊

Who became a king when he was a little
child? *Josiah.*

2 KINGS 22:1

❊ ❊ ❊

Who received the first kiss mentioned in the Bible? *Isaac.*

GENESIS 27:26-27

* * *

Where are magicians talked about in the Bible? *Genesis.*

GENESIS 41:8

* * *

What did David do with Goliath's weapons after killing him? *He kept them.*

1 SAMUEL 17:54

* * *

How many sons did Gideon have? *Seventy-one.*

JUDGES 8:29-31,35

* * *

How many rivers flowed out of the Garden of Eden? *Four.*

GENESIS 2:10,14

* * *

Who was the first archer mentioned in the Bible? *Ishmael.*

GENESIS 16:16; 21:14,20

* * *

Who called himself "a dead dog"? *Mephibosheth.*

2 SAMUEL 9:6,8

* * *

What does the name "Wormwood" refer to? *A star that fell from heaven.*

REVELATION 8:10-11

* * *

How many proverbs did King Solomon know? *Three thousand.*

1 KINGS 4:30,32

✳ ✳ ✳

When Jacob first met Rachel, what did he do after he kissed her? *He wept.*

GENESIS 29:11,18

✳ ✳ ✳

How many songs did King Solomon compose? *One thousand and five.*

1 KINGS 4:30,32

✳ ✳ ✳

In what way did King Nebuchadnezzar act like an ox? *He ate grass.*

DANIEL 4:33

✳ ✳ ✳

Why was dove manure sold for food?
The country was under siege.

2 KINGS 6:25

* * *

What did the apostle John eat that gave him indigestion? *A little book.*

REVELATION 10:10

* * *

How long did Isaiah walk around naked? *Three years.*

ISAIAH 20:3

* * *

Jesus had four brothers and at least how many sisters? *Two.*

MARK 6:3

* * *

What did Nehemiah do to the men who had married interracially? *He tore out their hair.*

NEHEMIAH 13:23-25

* * *

Who was the first drunkard mentioned in the Bible? *Noah.*

GENESIS 9:20-21

* * *

Who had brothers named Joses, Simon, Judas, and James? *Jesus.*

MATTHEW 13:55

* * *

What did Samson do to 300 foxes? *He set their tails on fire.*

JUDGES 15:4

* * *

According to the Bible, what animal is cruel to her young? *The ostrich.*

JOB 39:13-17

* * *

What is the most used word in the Bible? *"The."*

* * *

How many times does the name Judas Iscariot occur in the Bible? *Ten.*

* * *

What does the phrase "Parbar westward, four at the causeway, and two at Parbar" refer to? *The placement of gatekeepers.*

1 CHRONICLES 26:18

* * *

How many times does the name Satan
appear in the Bible? *Fifty-three.*

* * *

What did two tribes build and call "Ed"?
An altar.

JOSHUA 22:34

5

Bible Trivia for the Humorist

What was the name of Isaiah's horse?
Is Me. Isaiah said, "Woe is me."

* * *

Who was the smallest man in the Bible?
Peter the disciple. He slept on his watch.

* * *

What did Noah say while he was loading animals into the ark? *"Now I've herd everything."*

115

Where in the Bible does it say that fathers should let their sons use the automobile? *Proverbs 13:24 (KJV). "He that spareth his rod hateth his son."*

* * *

What simple affliction brought about the death of Samson? *Fallen arches.*

> Has it ever struck you that the vast majority of the will of God for your life has already been revealed in the Bible? That is a crucial thing to grasp.
>
> Paul Little

Why were Adam and Eve kicked out of the Garden? *For raising Cain.*

* * *

Where in the Bible does it suggest that men should wash dishes? *In Second Kings 21:13 (KJV). "And I will wipe Jerusalem as a man wipeth a dish, wiping it, and turning it upside down."*

✳ ✳ ✳

Why was Moses the most wicked man in the Bible? *Because he broke the Ten Commandments all at once.*

✳ ✳ ✳

What man in the Bible spoke when he was a very small baby? *Job. He cursed the day he was born.*

To what greater inspiration and counsel can we turn than to the imperishable truth to be found in this treasure house, the Bible.

Queen Elizabeth

At what time of day was Adam born?
A little before Eve.

* * *

What man in the Bible had no parents?
Joshua the son of Nun.

* * *

Where is tennis mentioned in the Bible?
When Joseph served in Pharoah's court.

* * *

How did Jonah feel when the great fish
swallowed him? *Down in the mouth.*

* * *

Where was Solomon's temple located?
On the side of his head.

* * *

Who was the fastest runner in the world?
Adam. He was first in the human race.

Bible study is like eating peanuts. The more
you eat, the more you want to eat.

Paul Little

How do we know that Noah had a pig in
the ark? *He had Ham.*

✳ ✳ ✳

Why did Moses cross the Red Sea?
To avoid Egyptian traffic.

✳ ✳ ✳

Why didn't they play cards on the ark?
Mrs. Noah sat on the deck.

✳ ✳ ✳

Who was the straightest man in the Bible? *Joseph. Pharaoh made a ruler out of him.*

> Unless we form the habit of going to the Bible in bright moments as well as in trouble, we cannot fully respond to its consolations because we lack equilibrium between light and darkness.
>
> **Helen Keller**

What has God never seen, Abraham Lincoln seldom seen, and we see every day? *His equal—Isaiah 40:25; 46:5.*

* * *

Which came first, the chicken or the egg? *The chicken, of course. God doesn't lay any eggs.*

* * *

What vegetable did Noah not want on the ark? *Leeks.*

* * *

What do you have that Cain, Abel, and Seth never had? *Grandparents.*

* * *

What was the first game mentioned in the Bible? *Hide-and-seek. Adam and Eve played it with God.*

No one ever graduates from Bible study until he meets its Author face to face.

Everett Harris

During the six days of creation, which weighed more—the day or the night?
The night because the day was light.

✽ ✽ ✽

Which animal on the ark was the rudest?
The mockingbird.

✽ ✽ ✽

What did Adam never see or possess, yet provided two of them for each of his children? *Parents.*

✽ ✽ ✽

What fur did Adam and Eve wear?
Bearskin.

✽ ✽ ✽

What kind of soap did God use to keep the oceans clean? *Tide.*

> The Bible will keep you from sin, or sin will keep you from the Bible.
>
> Dwight L. Moody

What is the name of the individual in the Bible who was perfect? *Mark. "Mark the perfect man, and behold the upright" Psalm 37:37 (KJV).*

* * *

It is greater than God and not as wicked as Satan. It causes death to the living who eat it, but can be eaten by the dead. What is it? *Nothing.*

* * *

Where in the Bible does it suggest that it is okay to be overweight? *Leviticus 3:16. "All the fat is the Lord's."*

I've read the last page of the Bible. It's all going to turn out all right.

Billy Graham

When a camel with no hump was born on the ark, what did Noah name it? *Humphrey.*

* * *

Where were freeways first mentioned in the Bible? *Genesis 1:30. "Everything that creeps on the earth."*

* * *

Why did the tower of Babel stand in the land of Shinar? *Because it couldn't sit down.*

✳ ✳ ✳

Who was the first man in the Bible to know the meaning of rib roast? *Adam.*

Bible reading is an education in itself.

Lord Tennyson

Where in the Bible does it talk about Honda cars? *Acts 1:14. "They continued in one accord."*

✳ ✳ ✳

When did Moses sleep with five people in one bed? *When he slept with his forefathers.*

✳ ✳ ✳

What was the first theatrical event?
Eve's appearance for Adam's benefit.

* * *

Why are there so few men with whiskers
in heaven? *Because most men get in by a
close shave.*

* * *

Who first introduced a walking stick?
*Eve...when she presented Adam with a
little Cain.*

* * *

Where did Noah strike the first nail in
the ark? *On the head.*

* * *

Why was Adam's first day the longest?
Because it had no Eve.

* * *

How long of a period of time did Cain hate his brother? *As long as he was Abel.*

* * *

Why was Job always cold in bed?
Because he had such miserable comforters.

* * *

At what season of the year did Eve eat the forbidden fruit?
Early in the fall.

* * *

On the ark, Noah got milk from the cows. What did he get from the ducks?
Quackers.

* * *

Where did the Israelites deposit their money? *At the banks of the Jordan.*

* * *

Which prophet became a space traveler?
Elijah. He went up in a fiery chariot.

* * *

What city was named after something on
a car? *Tyre.*

* * *

When Noah landed on Mount Ararat, was
he the first one out? *No. He came forth out
of the ark.*

* * *

When is the first math problem mentioned
in the Bible? *When God divided light from
darkness.*

* * *

When is the second math problem mentioned? *When Adam and Eve went forth
and multiplied.*

* * *

Why did Noah punish the chickens on the ark? *Because they used fowl language.*

✳ ✳ ✳

Who ate the most expensive meal in the Bible? *Esau. It cost him his birthright.*

✳ ✳ ✳

What do Matthew and Mark have that Luke and John do not have? *The letter "a" in their names.*

✳ ✳ ✳

What made Abraham so smart?
He knew a Lot.

✳ ✳ ✳

When was the Red Sea very angry?
When the children of Israel crossed it.

✳ ✳ ✳

Why do you think Jonah could not trust the ocean? *Because there was something fishy in it.*

* * *

What does God both give away and keep at the same time? *His promises.*

* * *

What did the skunks on the ark have that no other animals had? *Baby skunks.*

* * *

How do we know that the disciples were very cruel to the corn? *Because they pulled its ears.*

* * *

How many animals could Noah put into the empty ark? *One. After that the ark would not be empty.*

* * *

Which book in the Bible is the "counting" book? *Numbers.*

* * *

Which animal on Noah's ark had the highest level of intelligence? *The giraffe.*

* * *

Which animal on the ark did Noah not trust? *The cheetah.*

* * *

Which Bible character was as strong as steel? *Iron—Joshua 19:38.*

* * *

What man in the Bible is named after a chicken? *Hen—Zechariah 6:14.*

* * *

What Bible character had a name that rang a bell? *Mehetable (Ma-hit-a-bell)—Nehemiah 6:10.*

* * *

Which bird on Noah's ark was a thief? *A Robin.*

* * *

Who killed a fourth of all the people in the world? *Cain when he killed Abel.*

* * *

How long did Samson love Delilah? *Until she bald him out.*

* * *

What is the name of the sleepiest land in the Bible? *The land of Nod—Genesis 4:16.*

✳ ✳ ✳

What did Noah call the cat that fell into the pickle barrel on the ark? *A sour puss.*

✳ ✳ ✳

What ages were the goats when Adam named them in the Garden of Eden? *They were only kids.*

✳ ✳ ✳

David played a dishonest musical instrument. What was it called? *The lyre.*

✳ ✳ ✳

How did Noah keep the milk from turning sour on the ark? *He left it in the cow.*

✳ ✳ ✳

Why did the giant fish let Jonah go?
Because it couldn't stomach Jonah.

* * *

If a man crosses the Sea of Galilee twice
without a bath, what would he be?
A dirty double-crosser.

* * *

What day of the week was the best for
cooking manna in the wilderness?
Friday.

* * *

If Elijah was invited to dinner and was
served only a beet, what would he say?
That beets all.

* * *

If a soft answer turns away wrath, what does a hard answer do? *It turns wrath your way.*

* * *

What is the golden rule of the animal world? *Do unto otters as you would have them do unto you.*

* * *

Samson was a very strong man, but there was one thing he could not hold for very long. What was that? *His breath.*

* * *

Why was Moses buried in a valley in the land of Moab near Bethpeor? *Because he was dead.*

* * *

What is in the wall of Jerusalem today that the Israelites did not put there? *Cracks.*

* * *

Why is *w* the nastiest letter in the Bible? *Because it always makes ill will.*

* * *

How did Joseph learn to tell the naked truth? *By exposing the bare facts.*

* * *

What food did Samson eat to become strong? *Mussels.*

* * *

Why did Moses have to be hidden in the weeds quickly when he was a baby? *Saving him was a rush job.*

* * *

If Moses would have dropped his rod in the Red Sea, what would it have become? *Wet.*

* * *

In what way does an attorney resemble a rabbi? *The attorney studies the law and profits.*

* * *

What's the difference between Noah's ark and an archbishop? *One was a high ark, the other is a hierarch.*

* * *

What are two of the smallest insects mentioned in the Bible? *The widow's "mite," and the "wicked flee."*

* * *

In the story of the good Samaritan, why did the Levite pass by on the other side? *Because the poor man had already been robbed.*

Other Books by Bob Phillips

*All-Time Awesome Collection
of Good Clean Jokes for Kids*

*The Awesome Book
of Bible Trivia*

*The Awesome Book
of Heavenly Humor*

*Awesome Good Clean
Jokes for Kids*

*Awesome Knock-Knock
Jokes for Kids*

*The Best of the Good
Clean Jokes*

Dude, Got Another Joke?

*Extremely Good Clean
Jokes for Kids*

*Fabulous and Funny
Clean Jokes for Kids*

*Good Clean Jokes to Drive
Your Parents Crazy*

*Good Clean Knock-Knock
Jokes for Kids*

How Can I Be Sure?

*How to Deal with
Annoying People*

Jolly Jokes for Older Folks

*Laughter from
the Pearly Gates*

Over the Hill & On a Roll

*Over the Next Hill
& Still Rolling*

*Over the Top Clean
Jokes for Kids*

*Overcoming Anxiety
and Depression*

*Super Incredible Knock-Knock
Jokes for Kids*

*The World's Greatest
Collection of Clean Jokes*

*The World's Greatest
Knock-Knock Jokes for Kids*

For more information, send a self-addressed
stamped envelope to:

Family Services
P.O. Box 9363
Fresno, California 93702